Loving A Mysterious Soul

Whispers of a Love That Almost Stayed

Abhishek Punyani

India | USA | UK

Made with ❤ on the BookLeaf Publishing Platform
www.bookleafpub.in
www.bookleafpub.com

Dedication

To the soul who felt like stardust and silence
This book is the echo of your laugh.
The shadow of your absence,
and the love I never learned to unwrite.

Preface

Some stories are not written; they are felt, they
arrive, slowly, like rain.
This is one of them.
"Loving a Mysterious Soul" is not just a book of
poems.
It is a map of quiet moments, unspoken
goodbyes, midnight confessions,
and the sacred ache of falling for someone you
were never meant to hold forever,
but loved as if you could.

Each phase in these pages mirrors a part of
my journey,
from the first glance that made the world
hush,
to the slow blooming of trust,
to the words we whispered when the night felt
safest,
to the echo that stayed long after she was
gone.

This book holds real memories,
the drives, the silence, the coffee cups, the
forehead kisses,

and yes, the heartbreak that still lingers like
the scent of rain on old roads.

I've poured myself into every line,
not to find closure...
but to remember her softly.
And maybe, if you've ever loved someone
quietly,
if you've ever waited for a reply that never
came,
or traced their name in your thoughts long
after they left—
Then perhaps these poems will feel like yours
too.
Thank you for holding this story in your hands.
And if somewhere in these pages, you find a
reflection of your own...
know that you're not alone.
— *Abhishek.*

Acknowledgements

To write this book was to reopen wounds, relive magic, and gather every fragment of a love that once felt infinite.
And yet, I never felt alone while writing it.

To **my family**, thank you for giving me the roots to feel deeply and the strength to turn that feeling into words. Your love has always been the quiet force beneath everything I create.
To my dearest friends, **Harsh, Tejas, Dhwani, Ishaan, Divya, Rahul, and Saurabh and few other who i cant name but would like to include the initials of their first name(A, S, C, U, R, J)**; thank you for always holding space for me. For listening without judgment, encouraging me without pressure, and reminding me that even heartbreak can become something beautiful. You've been my anchors through it all.

To **Sampada**, for the calm, the quiet presence, and the reminder that healing isn't always loud and straight forward; thank you for being part of the light that led me back to myself.

To **the special soul who inspired these pages, my**

"Starling". Thank you for being the kind of mystery that changed everything. You may never read this, but your presence breathed life into every poem. Your absence shaped the silence between them.

To the nights that didn't let me sleep,
the drives that kept me dreaming,
the silence that made me write,
I'm grateful for all of it.

And to every reader holding this book now,
I don't know your story, but I might know the shape of
love,
and the ache of watching it drift into memory.
Thank you for letting mine meet yours.

And finally,
to the version of me that kept writing through it all,
you made it.
We made it.
She was real.
And this... this is how I'll remember her always.
— *Abhishek*

When Stars First Whispered

1. She Entered Like a Whisper

I saw her where the sunlight danced,
In fleeting glows of sweet romance,
Her laughter was the melody like a summer rain,
It healed a place I didn't name.

Her smile; oh God, that gentle spark,
Lit every corner, when I use to chase the dark,
It wasn't loud, it didn't shout,
But somehow, it erased my doubt.

The world grew still, the noise grew small,
As if her **soul** had stilled it all,
One glance, and I was not the same,
Like stars had whispered out her beautiful **name**.

She didn't know, she couldn't see,
The way **her smile** unravelled me.
Not in a rush; just slow control,
She softly stepped into my heart & soul.

2. Where Her Presence Blossomed

She moved like dusk upon the sea,
A hush of golden reverie,
Not loud, not bright; but something deep,
That stirred the **soul** and woke my sleep.

She lingered where the stillness grew,
In twilight's hush, in morning dew,
In echoes soft the stars once made,
In every place where light would fade.

I saw her not in things she wore,
But in the hush just past the door,
In candlelight and distant chimes,
In words that slipped between the lines.

And though she never called my name,
She knew the wind; it moved the same.
I loved her from a place unknown,
A quiet space she made her own.

3. When Words First Touched

It wasn't much; Just a simple "hi,"
Yet stardust flickered in the sky,
As if the **moon** had held its breath,
To feel what stirred in silence left.

Her voice; OH a spell the dusk had cast,
Soft as the wind that wanders past,
It held the warmth of firelight,
And all the magic born of night.

We spoke of skies and fleeting days,
Of little things and hidden rays,
But underneath, a current ran.
A pull too deep to understand.

Her laugh; My God That Laugh!
A bell from far-off lands,
It echoed deep like held-out hands,
And with each glance, the air would glow,

As if the stars began to show.

It wasn't much; but hearts had stirred,
Between each glance and quiet word,
A single spark, a soft command:
The universe had kissed my hand.

4. In Smoke and Sips

We wandered streets the **moon had kissed,**
In quiet talks and morning mist,
With coffee warm in trembling hands,
And steps that danced on shifting sands.

She lit a cigarette like art,
Each flick a window to her heart,
The smoke rose slow; a silver veil,
Between her soul and fairytales.

We didn't speak of love too loud,
Just shared our truths beneath a cloud,
A laugh, a sigh, a glance that stayed,
Like poems where no rhyme was made.

The world around would blur and fade,
As if for us, the night was laid.
And in that hush, I came to see,
That she was slowly **might bechoosing _me._**

No grand confessions, no bold vow,
Just coffee lips and moonlit now,
A gentle ache I couldn't name,
Yet knew I'd never feel the same.

5. She Spoke in Shadows

She didn't speak in certain terms,
But in the way her fingers turned
The sugar in her coffee cup,
Like stirring thoughts she'd locked up.

She looked at skies, not into eyes,
As if her truth lived in disguise,
But still, I watched her **soul unfold,**
In every whisper she controlled.

A cigarette between her lips,
A smirk, a sigh, a sip; **My God just like an Eclipse.**
She hid behind her gentle flame,
And dared me not to ask her name.

Yet still I stayed, and matched her pace,
With quiet hands and patient grace,
I didn't ask, I didn't press;
Some hearts require tenderness.

And though the night was growing thin,
She let a little silence in,
Where something soft began to grow;
A wordless trust, a subtle glow.

6. Where Her Laughter Lived

Her **laugh** was not a roaring thing,
No thunder crash, no golden ring,
But soft; like rain on rooftop tin,
That made the storm feel safe within.

It wrapped around my weathered soul,
A warmth that made the broken whole,
And in that sound, so light, so free,
I found a home inside of *me*.

Her soul; it didn't blaze or burn,
It didn't beg the world to turn,
But rested like a gentle tide,
That pulled me in, then stayed beside.

She didn't speak of peace aloud,
She simply walked beneath a cloud,
And yet, when near, the chaos ceased,
As if her silence **whispered *peace*.**

And in that laugh, and in that gaze,
I found myself in softer ways,
Not lost, not chained, not made to roam,
Just standing still, and feeling... home.

7. Numbers and Nervous Smiles

I asked, half-laughing, half-afraid,
Not sure if stars would let it stay,
She smiled, that tilted, teasing kind,
And typed her number in my mind.

No paper, no dramatic flair,
Just **digits** floating in the air,
Yet when I left, my fingers shook,
Like I had touched an unread book.

I waited, paused, rewrote, deleted,
Every line felt incomplete yet heated.
Then finally, I let it send,
A **"Hey, it's me"**, no need to pretend.

And hours passed like dripping stars,
Till ***her name lit up***, and healed old scars.
No song, no spark, no sudden flame,
Just soft hello, that whispered my name.

8. The One She Painted in

Words

We wandered where the city slept,
With stars above and secrets kept.
A cigarette between her lips,
Her coffee warm, her mind adrift.

She spoke of things she'd never touched,
Of lives unlived, of love too much.
A house where jasmine climbs the gate,
A moonlit road, a twist of fate.

"I want a man," she softly said,
"Whose soul outshines the stars overhead.
So gentle, even storms would part,
To kiss the stillness of his heart."

"A light so soft, the dark would blush,
A voice that calms the world to hush."
She smiled like she was seeing him,
Some spectral shape in twilight's hymn.

I watched her sketch a dream so wide,
And wondered if I stood inside.
But silence held me by the sleeve,
For some dreams aren't for us to grieve.

9. The Night She Doubted Fate

Beneath a sky of quiet fire,
She sat like dusk, half hope, half tire.
The stars were speaking, soft and slow,
Of things she feared she'd never know.

"I want to build," her whisper came,
**"Not castles, just a steady flame.
A life that leans, not breaks, with time,
A soul that answers mine in rhyme."**

Her eyes were lakes of echoed ache,
Reflecting all she dared not fake.
"I've loved," she said, **"and I have lost.
I've paid for dreams, and learned their cost."**

Then, with a glance that stilled the air:
**"I think we all have soulmates, there;
Somewhere across this spinning sphere.
Or maybe mine was already here."**

The wind grew still, the night stood long,
As if the stars had heard her wrong.
And yet I knew, right then, right there,
I wished her soul would choose to dare.

10. She Believed in Forever, Sometimes

She held forever in her hands,
Like falling dusk, like shifting sands.
She spoke as though the stars would wait,
But fate, she feared, was always late.

Her voice, a hymn of silent wars,
Her dreams, once gods, now closing doors.
And still she hoped, with all her might...
That love could bloom again from night.

11. Through the Glass of Her Silence

She sat with thoughts like distant stars,
Just out of reach, behind faint bars.
Her gaze was fixed on something far,
Not sky, not sea, but some old scar.

She never spoke when silence grew,
Just stirred her drink and blinked the blue.
But oh, the tales her stillness told,
In shadows soft and glimmers bold.

Her hands would move like drifting snow,
As if they wrote what lips won't show.
A sigh would slip, a shoulder bend,
And worlds would bloom and break and mend.

She wore her silence like a veil,
Of ancient myths and moonlight pale.
A sacred hush the stars would keep,
A quiet only dreamers seek.

I watched her like a prayer half-said,
With words I dared not give or shed.
For silence, when it's shaped like her,
Becomes the place where wishes stir.

And though I never held her thought,
Each glance she gave, an echo caught.
And in that hush I came to know,
Some souls speak loud in whispers low.

In the Gravity of Her

12. Conversations Like Rain

We started slow, a word, a phrase,
Then lost in hours, nights and days,
The kind of talks that wander deep,
Where laughter wakes, and wounds still sleep.

We spoke of **dreams and songs and skies**,
Of past goodbyes and almost-cries,
And though we barely touched at all,
It felt like letting armor fall.

Each message like a thread we spun,
Two souls just walking toward the sun,
We didn't rush, we didn't race,
We found the magic in the pace.

And sometimes, silence spoke the most;
A typing dot, a missed word's ghost,
Yet still I stayed, and she stayed too,
And built a bridge from **"me" to "you."**

13. The Way She Said My Name

She said my name like it was hers,
Like something stitched in summer swerves.
No thunder rolled, no music played,
Just soft as breath and gently laid.

She didn't sing, she didn't try,
Just let it float beneath the sky.
But still, it hit like whispered prayer,
As if the stars had placed it there.

A simple sound, no gilded gold,
Yet warmer than my hands could hold.
And though I'd heard it all my life,
That night, it cut me like a knife.

She said it once, then looked away,
Not knowing hearts can lose their way
On syllables so barely stirred,
A world was born inside that word.

And ever since, it feels the same,
Each time I hear her say my name,
Like I belong, like I've been seen...
Like I'm the line in someone's dream.

14. The Name Only I Would Use

It slipped one day; a soft intentional mistake,
A playful name I didn't fake,
It wasn't planned, or made to charm,
Just fell from lips that meant no harm.

She laughed, then paused, a curious smile,
As if she'd let it stay awhile,
No protest, just a tilted head,
And cheeks that slowly **blushed to red.**

I called her *"Starling,"* just like that,
A name the moon would whisper back,
It fit the way she lit the skies,
And tucked the world behind her eyes.

No one else would call her so,
It wasn't loud, it wasn't show,
But now that name, that quiet sign,
Became a verse that felt like ***mine.***

15. She Danced Without Music

She moved with no sound, no command,
Just twilight humming through her hands.
A spin, a sway, then slowing down,
Like dreams that tiptoe through the town.

No rhythm told her where to be,
She danced as if the air was sea.
Each step a ripple, slow and wide,
A comet tracing love and tide.

The world forgot its every sound,
As **moonlight wrapped her** like a gown.
No music played, yet still she swayed,
A hymn the stars themselves had made.

And I just stood, without a word,
Afraid to breathe, afraid she'd blur.
She wasn't dancing just for show,
But for the parts no one could know.

Her eyes were closed, her arms like wings,
She touched the dark with softer things.
The hush became a holy place,
As if I saw her soul in grace.

Then in the quiet, as she turned,
And every constellation burned,
I said, half-lost in heaven's gaze:
"Starling... you dance like a river of Milky Way
Flowing between the stars you sway."

16. The Miles That Bought Us Close

The sky was soft, a fading blue,
And every mile just led to *you*,
The wind was light, the road was bare,
But something sacred filled the air.

We stopped for cones, your favorite kind,
You took one bite, then changed your mind,
Vanilla swirled with cherry pink,
You laughed, and let the cold lips sink.

The songs we played were half forgot,
Yet now they live in every thought,
The night was young, the stars were shy,
But still, your laughter touched the sky.

You sat with one hand out the door,
Like chasing winds you knew before,
I watched you through the mirror's glow,
And felt the world begin to slow.

You spoke of dreams and simple things,
Of broken clocks and borrowed rings,
And I just drove, too full to speak,
Afraid my voice would come out weak.

And later still, when hearts replayed,
That night beneath September's shade,
The **28th** — a quiet flame,
That lit the dark and wrote your name.

I didn't know what love could be,
Until the road gave you to me.

17. When I Knew It Was More

You danced that night beneath the lights,
Like shadows twirling into flight.
And though the room was filled with sound,
I only heard your feet on ground.

We drove for hours after that,
With open skies and windows flat.
You laughed, and leaned your head just so,
And all the world began to slow.

I dropped you off and drove alone,
But couldn't shake your voice, your tone.
It echoed soft inside my chest,
A song I hadn't known I missed.

And days went by, but not that thought,
Of how your smile, unscripted, caught
My every sense and filled the air
With hints of jasmine in your hair.

We met again, just like before,
But this time something pulled me more.
You spoke, and I was not the same,
Each word you said became my flame.

Your eyes were oceans trimmed in light,
And I got lost without a fight.
Your voice, your laugh, your every breath,
Felt like a place I'd rest to death.

That's when I knew, it wasn't chance,
Not just a crush or passing glance.
It wasn't soft, or shy, or slow,
It was the kind that *had to* **grow**.

And though I smiled like all was fine,
Inside, I whispered: ***"She is mine."***

18. The Softest Fall

I didn't fall the way they write,
No crashing waves, no blinding light,
Just moments stitched in threads of gold,
That wrapped around me, soft and bold.

It happened in the way she spoke,
In pauses where the silence broke,
In how she breathed between her lines,
Like poetry the stars designed.

It happened when her eyes met mine,
And didn't flinch or flee or shine,
But stayed; like they had always known
That I was hers, and not alone.

I fell in how her fingers danced
While telling tales of days she chanced,
In how she sipped her tea so slow,
Like tasting life before it goes.

There was no cliff, no sudden scream,
Just her becoming every dream;
A gentle drift I couldn't stall,
And I, without a fight, did fall.

19. The Way the Silence Changed

We didn't speak the whole way home,
The road a thread, the stars a dome.
No voices stirred the midnight air,
Just breath and sky and weightless care.

You leaned on me, a drifting moon,
As twilight hummed its quiet tune.
Your lashes fell like wishes made,
Your head upon my shoulder laid.

And in that hush, the world withdrew,
As if the night had paused for you.
No music played, no time to chase,
Just stillness shaped in sacred space.

The silence wasn't made of lack,
But something vast that called us back.
It moved like winds the gods once stirred,
A thousand thoughts that needed no word.

I watched your dreams in shifting light,
Your soul asleep in velvet night.
And in that moment, soft and wide,
The stars moved closer to our side.

No prayers, no vows, no grand display,
Just you, just me, the Milky Way.
And in that seat, without a sound,
I felt the universe unbound.

20. Where the Night Held You

You texted me, just past twilight,
"Let's drive beneath the city light."
I said **"YES"** fast; like hearts just knew,
That nights like this are rare and true.

I brought you flowers, pale and small,
You smiled and said, **"You thought of all."**
You smiled and said **"Why you do this all?"**
We drove through streets half-lit, half-sleep,
With music low and stars knee-deep.

You talked of dreams, then softly sighed,
Then leaned your head and closed your eyes.
And somewhere just before the dawn,
You drifted off; the world was gone.

I watched you sleep, one hand on mine,
While roads unwound like whispered time,
And morning rose in shades of gold,

Like promises we'd never told.

Outside your gate, you turned to me,
A silent hug, then set soul free.
I stood there long after you'd gone,
Still hearing echoes of your yawn.

You slept till noon, I never slept,
Just held the night in breaths I kept.
I missed your **scent**, your **sleepy laugh**,
The way you **hummed** and **leaned** and **laughed.**

I missed you like the moon missed day,
In quiet, soft, unspoken ways;
Not with despair, or tearful fall,
But with a love too big to call.

21. In Everything, Her

She's in the steam of morning **coffee**,
In **songs** that hum unconsciously,
In **pages** I forgot I knew,
She's woven in the world's soft hue.

She's in the **pause** between two words,
In distant trains and passing birds,
In every breeze that moves my skin,
She's there; **Always there in my heart**; without, and deep within.

She's in the **scarf** I see in stores,
The **books** I pick, the worn-out floors,
She's in the **jokes** I almost say,
And why I **smile** at skies so gray.

She's not a **thought** I chase or hold,
But one that's lived and softly told;
Like **prayers** that bloom without a sound,
Yet turn the silence sacred ground.

I don't know when the shift began,
When "***just a friend***" became the plan.
But now, each breath and every stir,
Carries a trace of only *her*.

22. The Moment I Almost Told Her

We walked beneath a sky half-woven,
Where even stars forgot what's spoken.
The moon hung low like it could hear
The quiet truth I held too near.

She laughed, then glanced, then touched her sleeve;
And I forgot how hearts should breathe.
The world stood still in silver hush,
And all I felt was rising rush.

I turned to her, the words half-shaped,
A vow the stars themselves had draped.
But then she smiled, not just at me,
But at some thought I couldn't see.

And just like that, I pulled them in,
The words that danced beneath my skin.
Not out of doubt, or fleeting whim,
But fear that love might make her dim.

My Thoughts?

"What if she saw too much too fast?
What if this moment couldn't last?
What if the light I placed in her
Was not the one she'd want to stir?"

So I just nodded, let her speak,
And memorized her blushing cheek.
For sometimes silence is the cost
Of saying what we fear we've lost.

And though I didn't speak that night,
My soul still whispered in the light:
*"I love you... but not just yet,
Your heart's a song I can't forget."*

Where Love Found Its Name

23. Before I Said the Words

The city blurred as I drove slow,
A detour from the path I know.
You called me late, your voice a flame,
And suddenly; the night became.

I picked you up, the **world felt still**,
Like every star bent to my will.
We found a place where roses climbed,
Where time stood back, politely timed.

The lights were low, your smile aglow,
A kind of peace the poets know.
I reached for you; our fingers met,
And something in me **leapt**, and yet...

I didn't rush. I took it slow,
And let my trembling spirit show.
Then breathed the words I longed to keep,
From where they bloomed, quiet and deep:

"I want to hold your hand for years,
And keep your laughter close to tears.
To learn your scars, your fears, your flame,
And whisper love through every name.

So here I am, with all I own,
No grand parade, just heart and bone...
Asking softly, if I may:
I love you, Starling — may I say?"

You looked at me with eyes so wide,
Then leaned in close and gently sighed,
"You may," you said, **"I'm yours to claim;**
With every tear, and every flame."

24. The Night I Stole Stardust

The drive back home was made of gold,
Of shared soft glances, stories told.
The world outside just slipped away,
As love lit up the darkened way.

You walked ahead, I watched your frame,
Like saying "***mine***" without a claim.
Inside, the quiet took its place,
And coffee steamed between our space.

You sat, and smiled, and played with steam,
While I just lived inside a dream.
Then slowly, gently, I drew near,
Your breath caught light, your cheeks turned clear.

You closed your eyes; a hopeful guess,
Expecting maybe lips, or less...
But love had planned a softer spell,
And in that moment, silence fell.

I held your hand with steady grace,
And brushed your cheek like sacred place.
Then **kissed your forehead**, soft and slow,
Where all my truest feelings go.

You didn't move, just let it be,
As time bowed down for you and me.
And as I leaned away so shy,
One secret act slipped right nearby:

I took your **scrunchie**, star-bound thread,
And wrapped it 'round my wrist instead.
A little piece, a sacred sign,
To say, from now, your soul meets mine.

25. The Scrunchie Still on My Wrist

The morning bloomed in shades of grey,
As I drove slow to start my day.
The city stirred in silent hum,
But all I felt was that you're gone.

The radio played that song we knew,
Our melody in shades of blue.
And just like that, your memory filled the space,
Your laughter, scent, your sleeping face.

My right hand resting on the wheel,
Still chasing echoes I could feel.
And then I saw it; soft and wide,
The loop of stars you left behind.

Your scrunchie, tied around my wrist,
A universe in woven twist.
The same you wore when night stood still,
When time bent soft around our will.

I pulled aside and let it play,
The song, the ache, the Milky Way.
And snapped a picture in the light,
Of wrist and thread, and love held tight.

I sent it to you with a line,
A thought too big for space or time:
"This isn't just a thread of cloth;
It's gravity, it's breath, it's oath.
It holds the stars, it holds my day,
A part of you that chose to stay."

"Your hair; like rivers made of light,
A Milky Way in silver flight.
And now, each time I raise my hand,
I hold a galaxy you planned.
So if you ask what keeps me near,
It's this: a loop, a laugh, a year.
A sacred sign upon my skin,
That I still carry you within."

26. The Chocolate by the Counter

The café hummed a lullaby,
With coffee steam and evening sky.
We sat where windows kissed the light,
And hearts grew soft in gentle night.

You spoke of dreams in **sips and laughs**,
I traced the curve of time that passed.
Your fingers danced around your cup,
Like every moment waking up.

A brush of hands, a glance too long,
The quiet buzz of something strong.
Romance hid in the candle's flame,
In how you softly said my name.

But love, that night, wore different shoes,
Not wrapped in words or grandest moves.
It came in chocolate, small and sweet,
Displayed beside the checkout seat.

You tugged my shirt; a little pull,
So soft, so shy, my heart grew full.
I turned around, you looked and said,
With eyes that always turned me red:

"Can I have this? Just this one?"
Your voice like morning's rising sun.
Not for the gift, not for the treat,
But how you asked; so pure, so sweet.

I smiled, already saying yes,
My soul undone by your request.
And as I paid, I held that bar
Like it was dipped in falling stars.

It was the first thing, ever so small,
You asked from me — and yet it all
Felt like the start of something more:
A key, a thread, an open door.

27. The Night I Told You Everything

The music faded, voices dimmed,
The world outside grew quiet, trimmed.
We found a room behind the noise,
Where silence spoke and hearts found voice.

You came in close; no words, just breath,
A sudden hug, so soft, so deathless.
I froze a moment, then gave in,
To warmth that touched beneath my skin.

No plans, no kiss, no light too bright,
Just holding you through velvet night.
And as you slipped into your dreams,
I whispered softly, threading seams.

The things I'd never said out loud,
The hopes that scared me, fierce and proud.
I told you how I saw forever
In just the way you tied your sweater.

You didn't hear, or so it seemed,
But maybe love still reached your dreams.
And when the clock touched morning's edge,
With sky aglow at window's ledge,
I kissed your forehead, still, unseen,
A prayer, a wish, a moment clean.

You never knew the words I said;
But I have lived them since that bed.

28. The Night She Held Me First

The stars were folding into dawn,
The world outside was barely drawn.
I'd just confessed, in whispered tone,
All the ache I'd once called home.

And there she lay, her breath like tide,
A sleeping peace I couldn't hide.
I watched her dream, her lashes still,
And felt my chest begin to fill.

Then suddenly, without a sound,
Her arms reached out and wrapped around.
She held me close, with strength so kind;
Like threads of moonlight tightly twined.

Her head pressed soft against my chest,
As if to hush what hurt the rest.
No words, no stir, no waking glance,
Just gravity disguised as chance.

And in that **hug**, the years unwound,
The ghosts grew quiet, pain unbound.
The weight I'd worn began to fall,
As if her sleep could cleanse it all.

A thousand wounds I'd tried to hide
Were kissed by stars and pulled inside.
She didn't know what she had done,
But I was healed before the sun,
"And she became my sun".

She was the answer dressed in dreams,
The salve to all my silent screams.
And from that moment, till the day,
She held me tight, and fear gave way.

So if love asks how I was found,
It wasn't in a shouted sound.
It happened in a sleeping grace;
Her arms, the stars, that quiet place.

29. A Morning Made of You

You woke like sunlight stretched in skin,
With dreams still dancing deep within.
My eyes were sore, but full of grace,
I'd watched the night light up your face.

Still tangled up in warmth and thread,
Your cheek pressed soft against my chest,
The hush between us sang so loud,
No need for words, no room for doubt.

Your smile, a fragile, blooming thing,
Made every morning start to sing.
You blushed and turned your gaze away,
As if I caught your soul that day.

We stayed like that, like frozen time,
While phones kept buzzing down the line.
But no call held what we had here,
This moment built from calm and near.

Cuddled like penguins, cheek to cheek,
No script, no plan, no need to speak.
The room grew brighter, still we stayed,
Two hearts afraid to drift away.

And though the world began to call,
That morning carved into my soul's wall.
For I fell deeper, sweet and true;
In that soft hour...
Just holding you.

30. Where Her Fears Unfolded

We sat beneath a sky so still,
As if the stars had bent their will.
No constellations dared to speak,
Just her, and all she tried to keep.

A bottle clinked, her breath grew low,
And time forgot where it should go.
She poured her heart, without disguise,
A sea of storms behind her eyes.

She spoke of ghosts with living names,
Of love that left and left its flames.
Of friends who vanished into air,
And kin who loved her unaware.

She said, ***"I've trusted shards and dreams,
And every one unraveled seams."***
"Now trust," she sighed, ***"is something cursed;
The gift I gave, that always hurt."***

And I, I didn't try to mend,
I simply stayed, became the end
Of every story told in pain,
A lighthouse built to brave her rain.

I touched her hand but not her scars,
Let silence answer what she marred.
For love, real love, won't speak too soon,
It listens softly to the moon.

31. The Way She Looked at Me That Night

She reached before the world had turned,
To where soft candlelight still burned.
A place she loved, a sacred space,
Where dreams would rest and stars made grace.

I walked in slow, through velvet air,
With orchids whispering in their flare.
She turned; and time, as if aware,
Stood hushed beneath her mystic stare.

She didn't blink, she didn't breathe,
Just watched as love began to seethe.
Like I had stepped out from a spell,
And all her silence knew me well.

I held the gifts with trembling hands,
Her favorite things, from heart-spun lands.
And as I reached her final mile,
She wore the world behind her smile.

I kissed her hand, a sacred rite,
And stars around us sparked to light.
She woke, she blinked, she said my name,
But in her eyes, I saw the flame.

Not one of fire, fierce and fast,
But one that knew this love would last.

32. Of Coffee and Commitment

It wasn't vows or velvet scripts,
But morning light on parted lips.
The kind of love that doesn't shout,
It seeps in slow, then wraps about.

She brewed her coffee like a rite,
A potion born from morning light.
The kitchen hummed, her song was low,
A spell she cast in sugar flow.

No promises were carved in air,
Yet everything I needed... there.
The way she handed me my cup,
As if her soul had opened up.

She didn't say, *"I'll never leave,"*
But gods themselves began to believe.
And in that hush, that sip, that glance,
I saw forever get its chance.

No ring, no vow, no altar rose,
Just sleepy eyes and softened prose.
And love, dressed in its truest hue,
Was in the way she stirred it too.

33. I Wanted to Write Her Name in the Sky

Your love was never made for ground,
Too vast for walls, too wild for sound.
So I imagined ways to say
Your name not the one that the world know,
but the one only we know,
"Starling",
in stars, in skies, in sway.

I wanted to carve you in the moon,
And let the galaxies make room.
To tell the night, ***"This soul is hers,"***
And drape your name in astral verse.

If I could fold the sky in two,
I'd send its shimmer back to you.
A sealed envelope of space and flame,
Addressed with only just your name.

Your love; too radiant to cage,

Deserves the breath of cosmic stage.
I'd burn my voice into the sun
If it would prove that you're the one.

So when you ask what lives in me,
It's nebulae, it's stardust sea.
And every star that greets the blue,
Is me, forever naming you.
"STARLING"

34. The Last Time I Prayed for Us

It wasn't loud, it wasn't late,
No falling stars, no twist of fate.
Just me beside a window sill,
Where time stood soft, and heart stood still.

The light was low, the coffee cold,
But something in me took its hold.
A silence strange, a breath too deep,
Like love had stirred while half asleep.

I closed my eyes, hands in a clasp,
As if the sky could feel my grasp.
Not for forever, not for fame,
But just the whisper of your name.

"Let this be real," I told the stars,"
"Don't let us drift to different cars."
"If she's the fire the heavens chose,
Then hold us fast, don't let us close."

I didn't ask for perfect days,
Or songs that only lovers praise.
Just more of this, your laugh, your breath,
The way you slept beside me, left.

The truth is, love like ours can bend,
But that night, I prayed:
"Let this not end."

And though you never heard me say,
That night I gave your name away,
To every star and sky and flame...
So they would know, and guard your name.

It was the last time I believed
That even prayers could help me grieve.

Echoes in the Quiet

35. The Space Between Your Words

You still replied, just not the same,
Your texts arrived without a flame.
No **"missed you"** tucked between the lines,
Just lowercase words and borrowed time.

I asked if **something weighed** you down,
You **smiled** it off, then looked around.
And I, too scared to break the spell,
Said nothing that could make you dwell.

We walked, but slower, step by step,
The silence longer where you slept.
You held my hand, but not too tight,
And left before the edge of night.

A call, a laugh, then sudden pause,
I studied you for every cause.
You laughed, but not the way you used,
It felt like joy had been excused.

The **love** was there, I knew it was;
But softer now, with little flaws.
And maybe that's how endings **bloom**,
Not in a storm,
But surprisingly in a room
Where hearts once sang
And now just hum;
Too tired to stay, too full to run.

36. The Things I Didn't Say

There were words I left in silence,
Folded neat beneath my breath.
Like notes I meant to hand to you
But watched them age to death.

I should've said you made me whole,
That even when I seemed alright,
I kept your name beneath my ribs
Like stars that never learned to write.

I should've told you I was scared,
Not of love, but losing you.
So I played it calm, I played it cool,
And lost the one who saw me through.

I never said how much you meant
When night would press against my chest.
I never said I dreamt of you
Even when I slept the least.

I never told you "**please don't go,**"
Though every nerve inside me screamed.
I let you think I'd be okay,
While hoping love was still unseen.

There were poems I never read aloud.
And letters that I never wrote.
Now they sit like prayers unsent,
Still sealed in ash and folded notes.

37. The Last Time I Held the Door

I came at midnight, like you said,
Blue orchids swaying near your head.
A quiet hug, a half-warm smile;
We hadn't driven in a while.

You stepped inside, and off we went,
The city sleeping, soft and spent.
Your laughter lighter, dim with strain,
As if the joy now wore a chain.

Still, on my wrist your **scrunchie** stayed,
A thread of all the love we made.
You looked outside more than at me,
As silence filled the in-between.

The road bent back to where it started,
Your voice grew tired, a bit cold-hearted.
You said **I changed**, that I was lost,
Too much of me had paid love's cost.

You wanted more than what I gave,
And I too late, too slow to save.
So outside that hotel, we paused;
Two hearts that knew the love was flawed.

I stepped out first, the door in hand,
Still trying, though I'd understand.
You hugged me soft, but not too tight,
Then whispered, ***"Goodbye Starling's Lover..."*** into the
night.

And as you walked, so sure, so slow,
You turned once more, as if to know.
From far, you asked, ***"Why linger here?"***
But I just smiled, and let it clear.

I didn't speak; just held the air,
And whispered low, ***"Remembering this. I'm keeping
this."***
The way you left, the way it missed.
The way I watched your back retreat,
With flowers crushed beneath my feet.

38. What Still Lives on My Side of the Bed

Your side's still neat, untouched, aligned,
Like you just stepped out for some time.
The pillow fluffed the way you kept,
I swear some nights it still feels slept.

My side, a storm of sheets and sighs,
Of tangled dreams and blinking eyes.
But even now, I shift and slide,
To leave you room... on the other side.

The scent of you has dimmed, not died,
It lingers near where you'd confide.
A whisper in the cotton thread,
Of all the things we left unsaid.

Sometimes I roll too far, then freeze;
Expecting legs, or laugh, or tease.
And realize love can haunt the space
Where someone once just touched your face.

The bed's too wide, the night too long,
But I still hum our favorite song.
And in the quiet, soft and true,
The bedsheets fold themselves like you.

39. The Apology I Practiced Too Late

I should've said it face to face,
Not tucked between the time and space.
Not carved in drafts I never sent,
Or whispered when the air was spent.

I practiced it a hundred times,
In morning walks, in traffic lines.
Each version softer than the last,
But none could ever undo the past.

I'm sorry for the nights I drifted,
For all the ways your trust was gifted.
And though I held it close, too tight,
I still let go without a fight.

I'm sorry for the quiet days,
Where silence grew in tangled ways.
For every smile I wore too late,
For answers shaped like empty plates.

I folded "**sorry**" into laughs,
Into my work, my darker halves.
I wrapped it up in "**I'll be fine,**"
When really, I was losing time.

You deserved more than I could name,
And all I gave was half a flame.
So here it is, not dressed in gold,
Just truth, a little bruised and cold:

"I'm sorry.
For what I did.
For what I didn't.
For what I hid."

40. Things That Still Remind Me of You

Your **scrunchie's** still on my wrist,
Not for fashion, not for show,
But because it feels like holding
One last thread that won't let go.

Orchids bloom in a corner stall,
The kind you loved in shades of blue.
I see them often, pause, then pass,
I can't buy them without you.

That café counter still remains,
Where once you tugged my sleeve and grinned.
A single chocolate by the till,
I look, I smile... but never spin.

That song? It hasn't left my head.
Still plays when mornings taste like rain.
And every note is laced with you,
A quiet joy, a quiet pain.

And even now, when **I close my eyes**,
When the world goes soft and slow,
I see you walking toward my soul,
The way you did, not long ago.

That **smile**, that step, that starry look,
The way your laugh began to rise...
You're not a ghost. You're something more.
You're the dream behind my eyes.

41. The Drive We Never Took

There's a road that winds past the city's edge,
Where we once dreamed we'd drive instead.
A plan we made on quieter days,
"Someday soon," in gentle haze.

We spoke of it like it was sure,
A path through rain, through something pure.
You'd bring the songs, I'd bring the night,
We'd chase the dawn with windows wide.

But someday never came at all.
The texts grew thin, the nights too small.
And when the chance finally appeared,
Your name was gone, your voice unclear.

Still, I went once. Just to see.
The sky, the turns, the road, the trees.
I drove in silence, played our song,
And every mile just felt... all wrong.

No laughter echoed in the seat,
No tangled hair, no tapping feet.
Just air where once your warmth had stayed,
A ghost that wandered, soft and frayed.

I passed the lake. I parked the car.
And looked beside me where you are.
Or were. Or might have been, in truth,
If love had kept its reckless youth.

Some drives don't need a sudden end.
They fade like roads that bend, and bend.
And now that path, once ours to claim,
Is just a whisper with no name.

42. Love in Past Tense

She was the voice I waited for
In empty halls and open doors.
She was the breath that filled my night,
The hand that made the dark feel light.

She used to laugh at every pun,
Called coffee dates her form of fun.
She tucked her dreams beneath her sleeve,
And gave me more than I believed.

She knew which songs would calm the rain,
Could name my moods before I came.
She read my silences like text,
And answered what I never said.

But now I speak of her like rain
That came, then left, then came again.
Her name, once loud, now feels like lace,
Soft, fraying, drifting into space.

And last week, I typed out a note,
A trembling thing my fingers wrote:

"Hey,
I know you might be busy now,
And I know I messed some things somehow.
But if you ever find the time,
Could you call? I need a bit of calm.
From someone who once called me friend..."

I hit "**send**" like it meant less.
But truth was folded in the rest.
I didn't want her just to talk,
I wanted time to turn and walk.

Back to the days where "**she and I**"
Weren't metaphors we left to die.
But past tense love can't change its place,
It only fades, with quiet grace.

43. I Keep You in the Weather

We used to walk beneath the rain,
With soaked-up shoes and no refrain.
You'd laugh and say the skies were kind,
Like clouds had secrets just for minds
That needed washing...
Hearts that burned.
And I believed in every word.

Now, storms don't feel like just a sky,
They feel like you, still passing by.

Today, the clouds began to swell.
A storm rolled in; I knew too well.
I stepped outside, past roofs and shade,
And let the heavens break and braid
Their tears with mine, like whispered proof,
That I still walk this world with you.

I didn't flinch, I didn't run.

I looked straight up, and met the sun
Behind the grey, behind the grief,
And cried, without a sound, relief.

The rain, oh love, it kissed my skin
The way you once did, soft within.
And every drop that struck my face
Was one more piece of your embrace.

I stood there, soaked in sacred ache,
Remembering each smile we'd make.
Each time we danced in quiet storm,
Two souls in rain, refusing form.

You're not the lightning in the sky.
You're not the thunder passing by.
You're every raindrop on my sleeve,
The part of you I'll never leave.

44. The Messages I'll Never Send

There are messages still in my phone,
Unread by you, yet not unknown.
I never sent them, never tried,
Just let them sit, unsent, un-cried.

One was for Valentine's; a day
I used to joke would go your way.
I wrote:

"Happy Valentine's Day, Starling.
If today's for sweet things, you top the chart.
You make life louder, stranger, art.
And when you sit beside me while I drive,
I barely keep this car alive.
Hope today brings smiles and spark,
Maybe a walk with me near dark?
Sending love, or stealing some,
From the one you leave undone."

I saved it, stared, then closed the thread.
The heart felt loud, the fingers dead.
You weren't mine to send it to,
Not anymore, though it still feels true.

There are more: a "**Happy New Year**" draft,
A "**Miss you**" typed, then overwritten fast.
A "**Saw this and thought of your laugh,**"
All paused between **what was** and **what passed**.

And still they sit, those unsent sighs,
Each one a whisper love denies.
They say the things I couldn't bear,
That you were once, and still are, *there*.

45. When the Silence Answered Back

I tried once more, though I knew the truth;
That echoes don't return to youth.
But still I called. Still let it ring.
Still hoped the void would say **something**.

It wasn't late. It wasn't wrong.
I chose my words, kept them soft, not long.
Just one more chance, one final thread,
A whisper sent, not raised, not bled.

I watched the screen the way you wait
For stars to blink or skies to break.
And all I heard was nothing there,
No breath, no word, no weighted care.

No answer came. Not "**Hey,**" not "**Why.**"
Not even rage, not even **goodbye**.
Just silence wrapped in static air,
The kind that crushes, not that spares.

And oh, it hurt, not like a flame,
But like forgetting your own name.
Like losing track of who you are
Because the voice that knew you...
Is now too far.

That's when I knew,
You'd heard me once,
In every call, in every front.
But now you chose to not come back,
And silence answered
what I lacked.

46. What I Told the Wind About You

I sat alone in the dark tonight,
With smoke in lungs and no more light.
A drink half full, my silence more,
As shadows slipped across the floor.

No one to see, no need to lie,
Just me, the wind, the starless sky.
And in that stillness, I confessed
What I had hidden from the rest.

I said;

*"I didn't love her 'cause she shone,
Or for the way she stood alone.
Not for the eyes that caught the rain,
Or smile that dulled a thousand pains.*

*I loved her like you love your breath,
Unnoticed, needed... even in death.*

She wasn't loud, she wasn't flame,
She was the calm that knew my name.

She brought back life where I had none,
Made love a place I could become.
A trust I thought I'd never know,
She gave it back... then let it go.

If someone asked, I'd tell them true,
How we first met, the sky's deep blue.
The shape of her laugh, the tilt of her nose,
The way my world bloomed like a rose.

I don't know when I fell so deep,
But stars can fall while skies still sleep.
And if love was meant to stay awhile,
I swore to carry hers in mine."

Then I lit another match and sighed,
And let the trees and stars decide
If they would take those words away,
And find her,
With something left to say.

47. Before We Let Go, If Only Once More

Still!
If your heart can hear me now,
Across the ache, beyond the vow,
Through all the noise this world may send,
Through all the things we couldn't mend,

If there's a place where stars still bend,
Where broken things find light again...
Not with a storm, but soft decay,
Then let my soul reach out and say,

"I wish we had just one more night,
One last drive beneath soft streetlight.
One final ride through silent skies,
Where I could see the stars in your eyes.

Maybe one more cup, one last café,
A gentle laugh to end the day.
I'd hold your hand, not say too much,

Just memorize the way we touch.

One more hug, one last goodbye,
One more look beneath the sky.
A kiss not rushed, not just for show,
But one that tells you all I know."

No grand reply, no need to sway...
Just this one breath I send your way:

47. Before We Let Go, If Only Once More

Starling, I loved you.
I still do.
All I have is one last thing to say,
Come on,
Please stay.

Final Message: The Yearning Heart

In a world of nearly eight billion souls, we find ourselves mourning the loss of just one. We ache, we break, and we hold on to the ghost of what once was. But for how long? The heart, fragile yet resilient, will always yearn; not just for love, but for a love that stays.

True companionship is not found in longing alone, nor in the desperate grasp for what has already slipped away. It is found in the quiet understanding between two souls who choose each other, not out of need, but out of harmony. Love should not just suit one of us; it must belong to both.